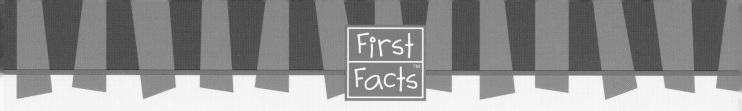

First Facts™

Holidays and Culture

Diwali

Hindu Festival of Lights

by June Preszler

Consultant:
Keith Snodgrass
Associate Director and Outreach Coordinator for South Asia Center
University of Washington, Seattle

Capstone
press®
Mankato, Minnesota

First Facts is published by Capstone Press,
151 Good Counsel Drive, P.O. Box 669, Mankato, Minnesota 56002.
www.capstonepress.com

Library of Congress Cataloging-in-Publication Data
Preszler, June, 1954–
    Diwali : Hindu festival of lights / by June Preszler.
    p. cm.—(First facts. Holidays and culture)
    Summary: "Describes the history and meaning of Diwali and how it is celebrated today"—
Provided by publisher.
    Includes bibliographical references and index.
    ISBN-13: 978-0-7368-6395-7 (hardcover)
    ISBN-10: 0-7368-6395-8 (hardcover)
    1. Divali—Juvenile literature. I. Title. II. Series.
BL1239.82.D58P74 2007
294.5′36—dc22   2006002828

Editorial Credits
Shari Joffe, editor; Biner Design, designer; Juliette Peters, set designer; Jo Miller, photo researcher;
    Scott Thoms, photo editor

Photo Credits
AP/Wide World Photos, 15, 18–19
Art Directors/Helene Rogers, 1, 9, 11, 20
Aurora/David H. Wells, 16
Capstone Press/Karon Dubke, 21
Corbis/Arvind Garg, 12–13; Chris Hellier, 7; Reuters, cover; Reuters/Ajay Verma, 4–5
Getty Images Inc./AFP/Indranil Mukherjee, 17; AFP/Narinder Nanu, 14

1 2 3 4 5 6 11 10 09 08 07 06

Table of Contents

Celebrating Diwali

All across India, bright lights flicker in homes and yards. Children eagerly light clay lamps and candles. Families and friends share cards, gifts, and sweets. Cities seem to glow during Diwali, the Festival of Lights.

Fact!

Hindu people throughout the world celebrate Diwali. In India, it is the biggest festival of the year and is enjoyed by people of all religions.

What Is Diwali?

Diwali marks the start of the **Hindu** New Year. To start the new year right, families clean their homes. They buy new clothing and jewelry.

During Diwali, Hindu people **honor** their gods and goddesses. They praise wealth and goodness. They give thanks for the people and things in their lives.

Fact!

Diwali is celebrated for five days in October or November during a new moon. There is no single Hindu calendar, so Diwali falls at different times in different parts of India.

Rama

Many people **worship** Rama during Diwali. Hindu **tradition** says that the demon king Ravana stole Rama's wife Sita. Rama fought to save her and defeated the demon. The Hindu believe that Rama was a great hero and the perfect king. His story is one of good over evil. It is an important part of Hindu **culture**.

Fact!

Diwali means "row of lighted lamps." It is said that people lit rows of lamps to welcome Rama back home after he beat the demon. Today, lights during Diwali stand for the power of good over evil.

Rama

Many people **worship** Rama during Diwali. Hindu **tradition** says that the demon king Ravana stole Rama's wife Sita. Rama fought to save her and defeated the demon. The Hindu believe that Rama was a great hero and the perfect king. His story is one of good over evil. It is an important part of Hindu **culture**.

Fact!

Diwali means "row of lighted lamps." It is said that people lit rows of lamps to welcome Rama back home after he beat the demon. Today, lights during Diwali stand for the power of good over evil.

The Five Days of Diwali

Each day of Diwali has special meaning and **customs**. On the first day, many people shop. It is lucky to buy something gold or silver. The second day honors the power of good over evil.

The third day is the actual day of Diwali. People share sweets and gifts. At night there are fireworks. The fourth day begins the new business year. On the fifth day, brothers and sisters honor each other.

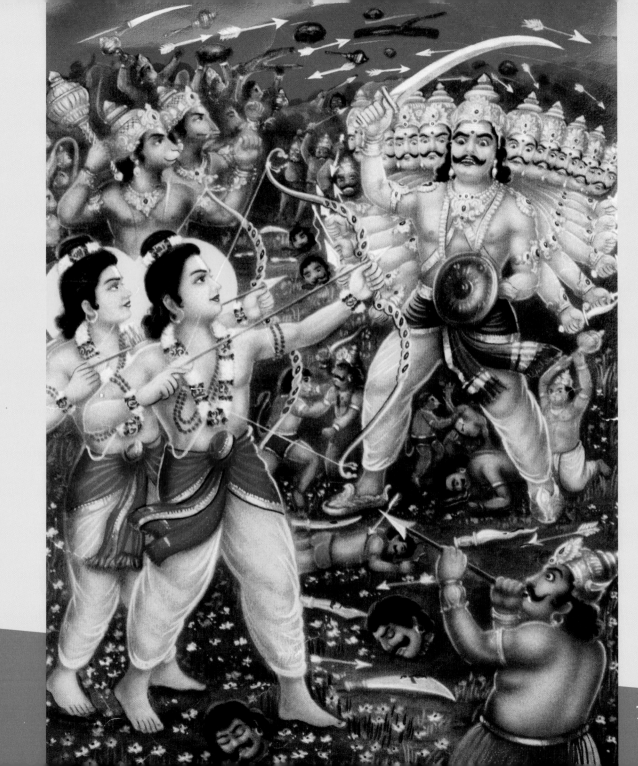

Lakshmi

Lakshmi

Lakshmi, the Hindu goddess of wealth, is honored on Diwali. People hope that she will bring them good fortune in the new year. They open their windows and light candles to invite her inside. They pray to her and offer her food, money, and flowers.

Fact!

Gambling is common during Diwali. Some people believe new wealth can come during Diwali.

Bright Night Skies

Fireworks light up the night during Diwali. Firecrackers explode. Rockets whiz across starry skies. Noisy, bright fireworks help keep evil away.

Fireworks have a joyful meaning, too. Bright and loud firecrackers help thank the gods for peace, riches, knowledge, and good health.

Rangoli

Art is everywhere during Diwali. People paint floors, walls, and doorsteps with colored paste. This beautiful folk art is called *rangoli*.

The paste is made from rice flour or crushed white stone. Rangoli spreads joy all around and makes a warm welcome for guests during Diwali.

Stop, Laugh, and Enjoy

The celebration of Diwali varies around the world, but one thing is the same everywhere. People take time to enjoy the good things in life. They look forward to new beginnings.

Amazing Holiday Story!

Today's busy world has changed how some people celebrate Diwali. At one time, people exchanged gifts in person during Diwali. Today, more and more people live far from loved ones. So, many people send Diwali cards and e-mail cards. Recently, the Google Internet search "Diwali greetings" was the second-most popular search worldwide during Diwali.

Hands On: Rangoli

During Diwali, women draw rangoli designs on doorsteps, courtyards, and temple entrances. The designs welcome friends and worshippers. Here is a simple rangoli design you can draw with chalk on paper. Later you might try drawing it on the sidewalk.

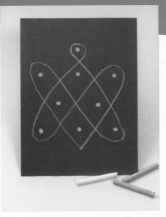

What You Need

white or light-colored chalk
black or other dark-colored construction paper

What You Do

1. Using the chalk, make the grid of dots and rows that you see at right. Make sure you keep the dots lined up and evenly spaced.
2. Now you are ready to draw your design. Begin at the top of the design and draw your shape without lifting the chalk.

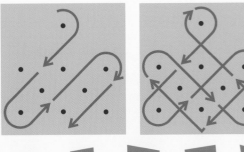

Glossary

culture (KUHL-chur)—a people's way of life, ideas, customs, and traditions

custom (KUHSS-tuhm)—a tradition in a culture or society

Hindu (HIN-doo)—describing Hinduism, a religion practiced mainly in India; Hindus believe they must act in harmony with universal laws and that various gods are different forms of the Supreme Deity.

honor (ON-ur)—to give praise or show respect

rangoli (ran-GOAL-ee)—chalk art designs drawn on floors or walls in India

tradition (truh-DISH-uhn)—a custom, idea, or belief passed down through time

worship (WUR-ship)—to express love or honor to a higher being

Read More

Gardeski, Christina Mia. *Diwali.* Rookie Read-About Holidays. New York: Children's Press, 2001.

Hughes, Monica. *My Divali.* Festivals. Chicago: Raintree, 2004.

Parker-Rook, Michelle. *Diwali: The Hindu Festival of Lights, Feasts, and Family.* Berkeley Heights, N.J.: Enslow Publishers, 2004.

Internet Sites

FactHound offers a safe, fun way to find Internet sites related to this book. All of the sites on FactHound have been researched by our staff.

Here's how:

1. Visit *www.facthound.com*

2. Choose your grade level.

3. Type in this book ID **0736863958** for age-appropriate sites. You may also browse subjects by clicking on letters, or by clicking on pictures and words.

4. Click on the **Fetch It** button.

FactHound will fetch the best sites for you!

Index

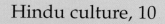